ALL ABOUT SPACE SCIENCE

ECLIPSES

Jessica Morrison and
Steve Goldsworthy

MEDIA ENHANCED BOOKS
AV2 BY WEIGL
ADDED VALUE • AUDIO VISUAL

www.av2books.com

AV² provides enriched content that supplements and complements this book. Weigl's AV² books strive to create inspired learning and engage young minds in a total learning experience.

Your AV² Media Enhanced books come alive with...

Audio
Listen to sections of the book read aloud.

Key Words
Study vocabulary, and complete a matching word activity.

Go to **www.av2books.com**, and enter this book's unique code.

Video
Watch informative video clips.

Quizzes
Test your knowledge.

BOOK CODE

T836496

AV² by Weigl brings you media enhanced books that support active learning.

Embedded Weblinks
Gain additional information for research.

Slide Show
View images and captions, and prepare a presentation.

Try This!
Complete activities and hands-on experiments.

... and much, much more!

Published by AV² by Weigl
350 5th Avenue, 59th Floor
New York, NY 10118
Website: www.av2books.com

Library of Congress Cataloging-in-Publication Data

Names: Morrison, Jessica, author. | Goldsworthy, Steve, author.
Title: Eclipses / Jessica Morrison, Steve Goldsworthy.
Description: New York, NY : AV2 by Weigl, [2017] | Series: All about space
 science | Includes index.
Identifiers: LCCN 2016054643 (print) | LCCN 2017004497 (ebook) | ISBN
 9781489658128 (hard cover : alk. paper) | ISBN 9781489658135 (soft cover :
 alk. paper) | ISBN 9781489658142 (Multi-user ebk.)
Subjects: LCSH: Eclipses--Juvenile literature.
Classification: LCC QB175 .M67 2017 (print) | LCC QB175 (ebook) | DDC
 523.9/9--dc23
LC record available at https://lccn.loc.gov/2016054643

Printed in the United States of America in Brainerd, Minnesota
1 2 3 4 5 6 7 8 9 0 21 20 19 18 17

032017
020117

Editor: Katie Gillespie
Art Director: Terry Paulhus

Photo Credits
Every reasonable effort has been made to trace ownership and to obtain permission to reprint copyright material. The publishers would be pleased to have any errors or omissions brought to their attention so that they may be corrected in subsequent printings.

Weigl acknowledges Getty Images, iStock, Alamy, and NASA as its primary image suppliers for this title.

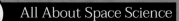

ALL ABOUT SPACE SCIENCE

ECLIPSES

CONTENTS

What Is an Eclipse?

An eclipse occurs when one object moves in front of another, hiding it from view. When a person wears a hat with a large brim to shield his or her eyes, the brim eclipses the Sun. Eclipses can also happen on a much larger scale. Many people are fascinated by these larger eclipses, such as a **lunar eclipse** or a **solar eclipse**.

In 1991, a total solar eclipse occurred over the W. M. Keck Observatory near the summit of Mauna Kea, Hawai'i. The observatory has two of the largest astronomical telescopes in use today.

In **astronomy**, an eclipse occurs when all or part of one **celestial body** is behind another one and is in its shadow. Most commonly, three celestial bodies, such as the Sun, the Moon, and Earth, are in line. Depending on the order in which they are in line, either a lunar or a solar eclipse may occur.

In the past, many people became frightened when an eclipse occurred. It can appear **ominous** for the Sun or Moon to be covered by a shadow. All eclipses, however, can be explained with science.

A total solar eclipse will occur on August 21, 2017.

END OF THE WORLD

The ancient Maya feared that an eclipse would lead to the end of the world. They prayed to the Sun God Kinich Ahau to battle the darkness and restore the sunshine.

The Hupa, a Native American tribe from California, believed that the Moon had many pets. When the Moon did not feed his pets, they attacked him and made him bleed. This explained the red color of the Moon during a lunar eclipse.

Solar Eclipses

There are three different types of solar eclipses. These are total eclipses, partial eclipses, and annular eclipses. The type of eclipse that occurs depends on the Moon's location in space.

A *partial* solar eclipse will occur on **February 15**, 2018.

In a total eclipse, the Sun appears to be completely covered. It looks like a black circle with only a thin halo of light around it. This halo is the region around the Sun called the **corona**. A total solar eclipse does not last for a long time. It is normally visible in any one spot for only about three minutes. A total eclipse occurs when Earth, the Moon, and the Sun are exactly aligned. In a total eclipse, the Moon's **orbit** takes it close to Earth.

A partial eclipse occurs when the Sun, the Moon, and Earth are almost but not exactly aligned. In a partial eclipse, only part of the Sun is covered by the Moon. The Sun appears to have a bite taken out of it.

In a total solar eclipse, the Moon appears large enough to totally block the Sun in the sky.

An annular eclipse happens when the Moon passes in front of the Sun but does not completely cover it. These eclipses occur when the Moon's orbit takes it far away from Earth. The Moon looks too small in the sky to completely cover the Sun. During an annular eclipse, a ring of sunlight surrounds the shadow of the Moon.

An **annular** eclipse is sometimes called a "ring of fire" because a bright ring of sunlight can be seen during the event.

The shadow the Moon casts on Earth during an eclipse has two parts. They are the **umbra** and the **penumbra**, or complete and partial shadows. As the Moon travels between Earth and the Sun, the area of Earth that is completely blocked from sunlight at some time during this passage is called the **path of totality**. The path, which covers about 1 percent of Earth's surface area, is usually 10,000 miles (16,000 kilometers) long but only 100 miles (160 km) wide. People in the path of totality are in the Moon's umbra. In areas outside but close to the path of totality, a partial solar eclipse occurs. These areas are in the Moon's penumbra.

An annular eclipse looks very different to a total eclipse, as the Moon does not fully cover the Sun.

Lunar Eclipses

Lunar eclipses occur during a full Moon, when the Moon usually looks like a complete circle of light in the night sky. These eclipses can be total or partial. In a total lunar eclipse, the Sun, Earth, and the Moon are aligned, and Earth's shadow completely covers the Moon. In a partial eclipse, they are almost aligned. Earth's shadow partly covers the Moon.

During a total lunar eclipse, the Moon does not become dark. It actually turns a reddish-orange color. This happens because some of the Sun's light still reaches the Moon even though it is completely within Earth's shadow.

On September 27, 2015, a supermoon and total lunar eclipse occurred at the same time. This will not happen again until 2033.

Sunlight is made up of different kinds of light that have various colors, including blue, red, and yellow. Some sunlight traveling past Earth during a lunar eclipse goes through Earth's **atmosphere**. During this passage through the atmosphere, the sunlight is separated into its different colors. The atmosphere acts like a lens and bends the rays of red light. It is the same effect that produces reddish colors during a sunset. As the red light is bent, some of it reaches the Moon while it is in Earth's shadow. The result is the reddish color viewers can see during a total lunar eclipse.

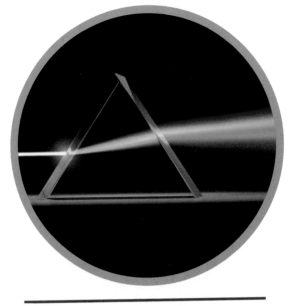

Different colors have different wavelengths, or the distances from one wave of energy to the next. Violet has the shortest wavelength and red has the longest.

The brightness of the Moon during a total lunar eclipse depends on weather conditions and the amount of dust in the atmosphere.

Orbits and Eclipses

Eclipses occur because celestial bodies are in motion. Some of them orbit another celestial body. Earth orbits the Sun, and the Moon orbits Earth. They travel in curved paths that are shaped like ovals. Earth takes one year to go around the Sun once. The Moon takes about a month to go once around Earth.

EARTH AND THE MOON'S ORBITS

Scientists today know the paths that Earth and the Moon take in their orbits. They know the speeds at which Earth and the Moon travel. Using this information, they can accurately predict the times and places at which eclipses will occur in the future.

SOLAR ECLIPSE

As Earth and the Moon travel in their orbits, at times the Moon passes between Earth and the Sun. When this happens, the Moon blocks sunlight from reaching a part of Earth for a short time. It casts a shadow on Earth. For people in this shadow, the Sun appears to be covered, and daylight may briefly turn into darkness. This event is called a solar eclipse.

LUNAR ECLIPSE

At other times as Earth and the Moon orbit, Earth passes between the Sun and the Moon. Earth briefly blocks sunlight from reaching the Moon. This event is called a lunar eclipse.

ECLIPSES PER YEAR

Every year there are four to seven eclipses of some type. This number varies due to the Moon and Earth's orbits.

PREDICTING ECLIPSES

According to the ancient Greek historian Herodotus, Thales of Miletus predicted that a solar eclipse would occur in 585 BC. Historians have confirmed that a solar eclipse did occur on May 28, 585 BC. If Herodotus' account is correct, then this is the earliest recorded predicted eclipse.

The solar eclipse interrupted a battle between the Medes and the Lydians. The eclipse was seen as a bad omen. Both sides laid down their weapons and declared peace. **Astronomers** can calculate the dates of past eclipses. This battle is one of the earliest historical events that can be dated to the day.

Eclipse Experts

Humans have been fascinated by celestial objects and events for centuries. Today, many countries have space exploration agencies to study them. The National Aeronautics and Space Administration, or NASA, was established in 1958. NASA is the United States' leading space exploration agency.

NASA studies both lunar and solar eclipses. In December 2011, NASA's Lunar Reconnaissance Orbiter (LRO) gathered data about how quickly the surface of the Moon cooled during a lunar eclipse. This data allowed NASA to map the terrain of the Moon more accurately, as flat surfaces will cool faster than rough surfaces. During solar eclipses, NASA can more effectively study the corona. Usually this layer is too bright to be studied, but during a solar eclipse, NASA can use both ground and space instruments to view the Sun while the Moon blocks some of the Sun's glare.

Elevation data from NASA's LRO is used to track the path of totality of eclipses, such as the total solar eclipse on August 21, 2017.

PLANETARY TRANSITS

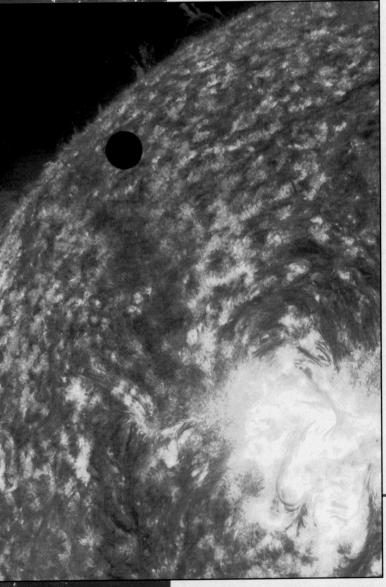

Not every eclipse involves the Sun, Earth, and the Moon. Sometimes, the planet Mercury or Venus, while orbiting the Sun, will pass in front of the Sun as seen from Earth. This type of eclipse is called a **planetary transit**. As a transit occurs, the planet is visible as a tiny dot traveling over the Sun's face. Planetary transits are rare. There are about 13 transits of Mercury every 100 years. Transits of Venus generally happen in pairs, with eight years between the two. Then, more than a century usually passes before the next Venus transit pair begins.

On June 5, 2012, NASA's Solar Dynamic Observatory (SDO) witnessed the transit of Venus across the face of the Sun.

Artificial Eclipses

The Sun is just one of billions of stars in the universe. It is very important to humans, however, because it is the closest to Earth. It is Earth's source of heat, and it controls the planet's climate.

Only the Sun's outer layers, which are called the solar atmosphere, can be seen. There are four parts of the solar atmosphere. They are the photosphere, the chromosphere, the transition region, and the corona, which is the outermost layer of the Sun. The corona is visible only during a total solar eclipse. At other times, other areas of the Sun are too bright for the corona to be seen from Earth.

Scientists are interested in studying the corona in order to learn more about the Sun. In the past, they needed to wait for an eclipse to view it. Today, there is an instrument called a coronagraph that can mimic an eclipse. A coronagraph is an attachment for a telescope that blocks out the direct light from a star. When it is used on the Sun, it allows scientists to view the corona.

The coronagraph was invented by a French astronomer named Bernard Lyot in 1930. From the Pic du Midi Observatory, high up in the French Pyrenees mountains, Lyot was able to take daily photographs of the Sun's corona. It is necessary to use a coronagraph at high altitudes as the diffusion of light through the atmosphere is less, allowing for a more distinct image.

In 1939, Bernard Lyot was awarded the Gold Medal of the Royal Astronomical Society.

Coronagraphs also allow scientists to view the Sun's prominences. Prominences, also known as filaments, are dense clouds of material that extend into the corona. They are often in the shape of a loop and usually extend for thousands of miles (km). The longest prominence on record was estimated to be more than 500,000 miles (800,000 km) long, roughly the radius of the Sun. Scientists are currently trying to figure out exactly how and why prominences are formed.

The total **lunar eclipse** of July 16, 2000, was one of the **longest** on record, lasting **106** minutes.

The speed of the **Moon** as it moves **across** the **Sun** is approximately 1,398 miles per hour. (2,250 km)

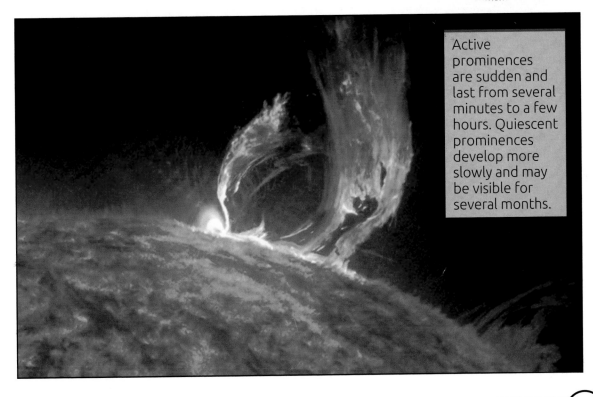

Active prominences are sudden and last from several minutes to a few hours. Quiescent prominences develop more slowly and may be visible for several months.

The Study of Space

By studying and observing eclipses, humans learned about the relative positions of Earth, the Moon, and the Sun. The ancient Greeks deduced that Earth was spherical by studying the Earth's shadow projected onto the Moon during a lunar eclipse. There are many areas of science that have benefited from knowledge gained by studying eclipses.

Many ancient cultures developed devices called astrolabes to find and predict the location of the Sun, the Moon, and planets. They were used to show how the sky looked from one place at a certain time. Astrolabes had moving parts that could be adjusted for the time and date. These instruments have sometimes been called "ancient computers."

A planispheric astrolabe is a map of the stars. The circles represent the path the Sun appears to trace over the course of a year, know an the ecliptic.

By the 17th century, more intricate astrolabes were used for navigation. Travelers used astrolabes to find the location of important constellations, from which they could judge their location.

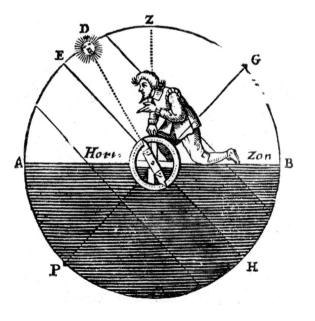

The astrolabe was commonly used until about 1650, when it was replaced with more complicated instruments such as the sextant. A sextant can be used to measure the angle between any two objects. It is used, for example, to measure the angle of the Sun or another celestial body above the horizon. Once the angle and time of day are known, it is possible to determine one's location and navigate safely.

Today, other types of navigation equipment, such as Global Positioning Systems, or GPS, also depend on knowledge of Earth's place in the cosmos. Navstar GPS in the United States has 24 main **satellites** that orbit Earth every 12 hours. These satellites provide navigational data from a far away view of Earth.

Today, GPS systems are often placed in cars, as they are more convenient for use while driving than a regular map.

Help from Eclipses

Scientists have gathered a great deal of valuable information by studying solar eclipses. Some of this information has enabled them to better predict when solar flares will occur. Solar flares are explosions in the Sun's atmosphere. The flares can reach Earth and cause damage.

For example, in 1989, a flare struck North America. A major electric-power grid in Canada was shut down for more than nine hours, causing 6 million people to lose electricity. The event caused an estimated $6 billion in damages. In February 2011, a powerful solar flare exploded. The most powerful seen in four years, it triggered a huge **geomagnetic** storm. A strong wave of charged **plasma** particles emanated from the Jupiter-sized sun spot and caused a disruption of radio waves in southern China.

MR. ECLIPSE

Fred Espenak is a retired astrophysicist who worked as an eclipse specialist for NASA. He is thought to be one of the world's leading eclipse experts. Born in 1953, Espenak became interested in astronomy and eclipses when he was a young man. Over the years, he has observed more than 20 eclipses in person. He has traveled all over the world in order to view them.

During his career at NASA, Espenak published yearly eclipse bulletins for scientists and other space enthusiasts. The bulletins provided eclipse viewers with detailed information about where and when every eclipse of the year would occur. He has also published several books about eclipses and is one of the world's leading eclipse photographers.

Although it may not last very long, one eclipse can provide scientists with enough information to analyze for months. Recently, scientists have been using eclipses to study changes in Earth's atmosphere. Some of these changes affect Earth's climate. The brightness of a lunar eclipse is rated on a scale called the Danjon scale, which goes from 0 to 4. The scale is named for Andre-Louis Danjon, an astronomer from France. By recording the brightness of a lunar eclipse, scientists may find clues about which chemicals are in the atmosphere. By studying how light reaching the Moon in a lunar eclipse now may be different from light reaching the Moon in the past, scientists can determine how Earth's atmosphere may have changed over time.

Fred Espenak's eclipse photographs have appeared all over the world in publications such as *National Geographic* and *Newsweek*.

Making the Grade

Studying eclipses and other astronomical events requires people to have very specific skills and knowledge. Viewing multiple eclipses also requires a lot of traveling, as eclipses occur in different parts of the world at different times. Specialists in many different branches of astronomy examine eclipses. They all need to use science and math.

ASTROMETRIST QUALIFICATIONS

EDUCATION
Astrometry is a specialized branch of astronomy. Astrometrists must have a minimum bachelor's degree in astronomy.

PERSEVERENCE
Astrometrists measure the distances and motions of celestial bodies, including planets and stars. They must be patient enough to gather data and study a question over a long period of time.

RESEARCH
Astrometrists are expected to share their findings with others. This involves writing academic papers on their research methods and results.

TECHNOLOGY
Astrometrists must be capable of using complex computer programs to analyze data.

TEACHING
Many astrometrists become teachers of astrometry. To become a professor of astrometry at a university, astrometrists must have a doctorate degree and academic work experience.

ASTRONOMER Astronomers spend much of their time analyzing the images and data captured by powerful instruments located on Earth or in space. Even with the powerful computers available today, astronomers may spend days, weeks, or more processing and studying the data and images delivered by their instruments. Some astronomers work at research institutes. Many others work at colleges or universities and teach as well as conduct research. Astronomers generally have a doctorate degree in astronomy or physics.

ASTROPHOTOGRAPHER An astrophotographer documents celestial events using photography. This requires a background in photography and specialized equipment. Telescopes, high-powered lenses, and advanced digital camera equipment are necessary tools. It is also essential to understand astronomy. The photos taken by astrophotographers are studied by scientists so as to better understand astronomical events. Most astrophotographers study photography and the techniques needed for capturing astronomical images.

ASTROPHYSICIST An astrophysicist is an astronomer who specializes in physics. Physics is the science of **matter** and energy. Astrophysicists study the physics of the universe. They might investigate the physical properties of a celestial body such as a star or a planet, or learn more about how stars form and change. Some astrophysicists research topics such as the origin of the universe or the possibility of life on other planets. People in this field usually have a bachelor's degree and a graduate degree in some area of math or science.

Eclipses from Space

Sometimes, it is possible for astronauts in space to view a solar eclipse from their space vehicle. They can watch from above as parts of Earth become dark. In order to view an eclipse, an astronaut must be over the right portion of Earth. Since eclipses last for only a short period of time, an astronaut must prepare in advance to be ready to observe and possibly take photographs of the event.

Just as people on Earth must often travel to experience an eclipse, so must astronauts. In 1966, one of NASA's *Gemini* missions changed its course in order to view a solar eclipse over the eastern Pacific Ocean. Viewing eclipses from space became somewhat easier once astronauts began to live in space stations for extended periods of time. For example, in 1999, the crew of Russia's *Mir* space station watched as an eclipse spread over Europe.

On March 29, 2006, the shadow of the Moon on Earth was visible from the International Space Station.

Today, astronauts from many countries are spending long periods of time in space aboard the International Space Station, or ISS. The ISS is the largest artificial satellite that has ever orbited Earth. Over time, astronauts on the ISS will have a number of chances to view eclipses. The information and photographs sent back to Earth will help scientists who study eclipses learn more about these events and the celestial bodies that cause them.

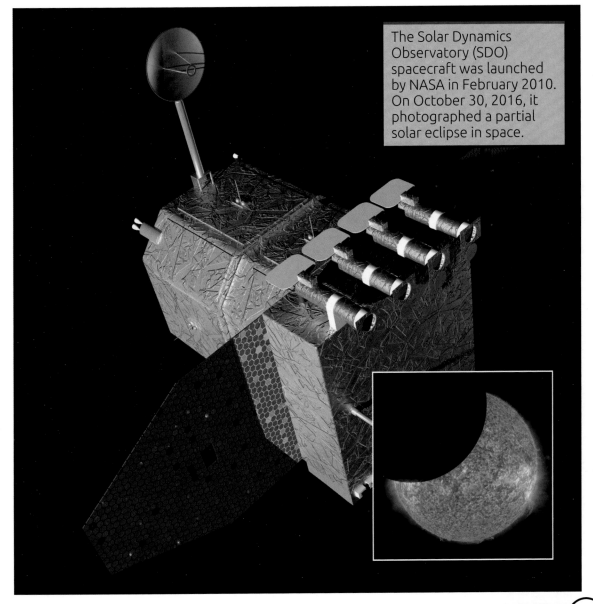

The Solar Dynamics Observatory (SDO) spacecraft was launched by NASA in February 2010. On October 30, 2016, it photographed a partial solar eclipse in space.

Viewing Eclipses

It is easy to observe a total lunar eclipse. As Earth passes in front of the Moon, the Moon will turn reddish-orange. It is more difficult to watch a solar eclipse. In order to view a total solar eclipse, a person must be at the right place on Earth. During a solar eclipse, the Moon's path of totality will cover only part of Earth.

People must be careful when observing a solar eclipse. Looking directly at the Sun can cause permanent eye damage and even blindness. A solar eclipse can be safely observed by watching the ground. As the sunshine hits the ground, viewers will see the light begin to fade. The Sun will become a shrinking crescent, and viewers will observe more and more darkness at their feet.

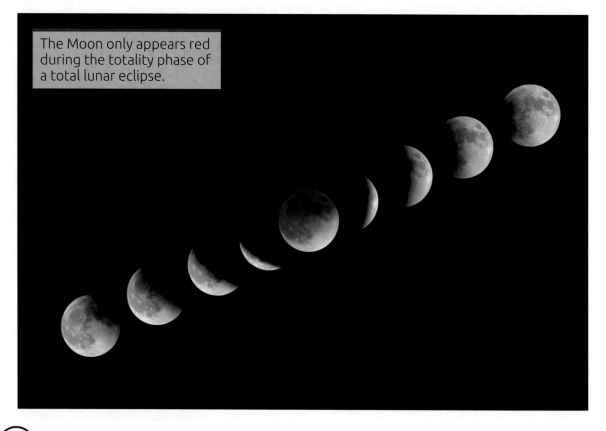

The Moon only appears red during the totality phase of a total lunar eclipse.

Another safe way to watch a solar eclipse is to view it indirectly using a piece of cardboard. Viewers can cut a small hole in the cardboard and set the cardboard on a window sill, letting the sunlight shine through the hole onto a wall of a room. As the eclipse occurs, the light on the wall will act as a miniature Sun. Viewers will see the eclipse on the wall.

It is also possible to buy eye-protection devices that are made to allow people to safely watch an eclipse directly. These devices usually have a thin layer of metal to reduce the intensity of the light. Eclipse viewers should not attempt to make eye-protection devices themselves and should never look directly at an eclipse unless they have proper equipment made for safe viewing. A total solar eclipse is visible somewhere on Earth about every 18 months. However, an eclipse will occur in the same place, on average, only about once every 370 years.

Mirrors can also be used to watch a total solar eclipse safely, by projecting the image onto another surface.

Eclipses Timeline

Throughout history, people have always been fascinated by eclipses. Early civilizations were baffled by eclipses and kept records of their appearances. This timeline highlights some of the key events in the study of eclipses that led to a deeper understanding of space and the solar system.

750 BC Ancient Chinese astronomers recorded 1,600 solar and lunar eclipses from this date onwards. After recording eclipses for 1,000 years, Chinese astronomers began to predict eclipses around 300 AD.

968 AD A total solar eclipse occurred on December 22, 968 AD. A contemporary chronicler, Leo the Deacon, documented the eclipse, commenting on the visibility of the outer layer of the Sun. This is the earliest confirmed account of the use of an eclipse to observe the solar corona.

3000 to 1500 BC The prehistoric monument Stonehenge was constructed in England. Little is known about the people who built the monument, but researchers believe that the stones were used to track eclipses. The number and arrangement of the stones allow for the tracking of the lunar cycle.

ECLIPSES IN MYTHOLOGY

There were many **mythological** explanations for eclipses. Eclipses were often seen as an evil omen. In many cultures, people would gather together to make noise during an eclipse by screaming or beating drums. They believed the noise scared the evil away. Not all cultures saw eclipses as terrifying, however. Some saw them as a chance to reconnect with loved ones, or as a time to reconcile differences. In either case, eclipses were always seen as a time of change.

In Inuit mythology, Anningan is the Moon god and his sister, Malina, is the Sun god. One day, the two siblings fought, and Malina ran away from her brother, running so fast that she became the Sun. Anningan chased after her, wanting to apologize, and became the Moon. Anningan often forgot to eat while chasing his sister, growing thinner and thinner. This explained the phases of the Moon. A solar eclipse occurred when Anningan finally caught up to his sister and embraced her to apologize.

1504 AD Christopher Columbus used his knowledge of eclipses to influence the Arawaks. He knew that there would be a lunar eclipse on February 29, 1504. He predicted that on this day, the Moon would rise "inflamed with wrath." The Arawak people were baffled when this prediction came true.

1919 AD Sir Arthur Eddington proved an aspect of Albert Einstein's 1911 calculations for the theory of general relativity. According to Einstein, the light from another star should be bent by the Sun's **gravity**. This effect is only noticeable during eclipses, so Eddington photographed the solar eclipse of May 29, 1919, proving Einstein's theory. After witnessing the solar eclipse, Eddington became a popularizer of Einstein's theory of general relativity, giving many lectures on the subject.

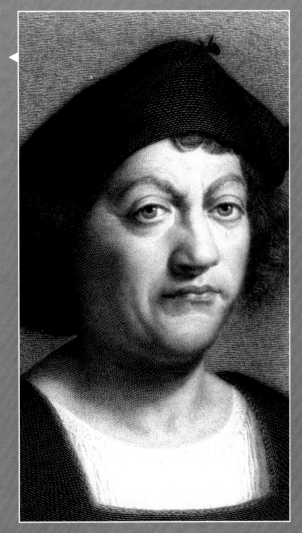

Ancient Norse tribes thought that an eclipse occurred when a pair of wolves ate either the Sun or the Moon. The two wolves who run through the sky are called Sköll and Hati. They are chasing the Sun and the Moon, called Sol and Mani. During a solar eclipse, the Sun appears as if the wolves have taken a big bite out of it. During a lunar eclipse, the Moon turns red, as if the hungry wolves have made the Moon bleed.

Eclipses Quiz

1

How many eclipses are there per year?

2

What is the outermost layer of the Sun called?

3

For how long is a total solar eclipse visible from one spot?

4

Why does the Moon turn red during a total lunar eclipse?

5

What type of shadow is the umbra?

6 What is the Inuit Moon god called?

7 What did Bernard Lyot invent?

8 When did Chinese astronomers begin recording eclipses?

9 How many transits of Mercury occur every 100 years?

10 How long do active prominences last?

Key Words

astronomers: scientists who study celestial bodies

astronomy: the study of planets, stars, and other objects in space

atmosphere: the layer of gases that surround a planet

celestial body: a natural object in space, such as a star or planet

corona: the outermost layer of the Sun's atmosphere

geomagnetic: of or relating to the magnetic field of Earth

gravity: a pull that objects or any bits of matter exert on one another

lunar eclipse: an eclipse that occurs when Earth travels between the Moon and the Sun

matter: any material or substance

mythological: imaginary

ominous: threatening

orbit: the path of a celestial body as it travels around another celestial body

path of totality: the path the Moon's shadow traces upon Earth during a total solar eclipse

penumbra: the shadow region outside an umbra

planetary transit: the passage of a planet in front of the Sun as viewed from Earth

plasma: a collection of charged particles containing approximately equal numbers of positive ions and electrons

satellites: objects in orbit around a planet or other body

solar eclipse: an eclipse that occurs when the Moon travels between Earth and the Sun

umbra: a region of complete shadow

Index

Log on to www.av2books.com

AV² by Weigl brings you media enhanced books that support active learning. Go to www.av2books.com, and enter the special code found on page 2 of this book. You will gain access to enriched and enhanced content that supplements and complements this book. Content includes video, audio, weblinks, quizzes, a slide show, and activities.

AV² Online Navigation

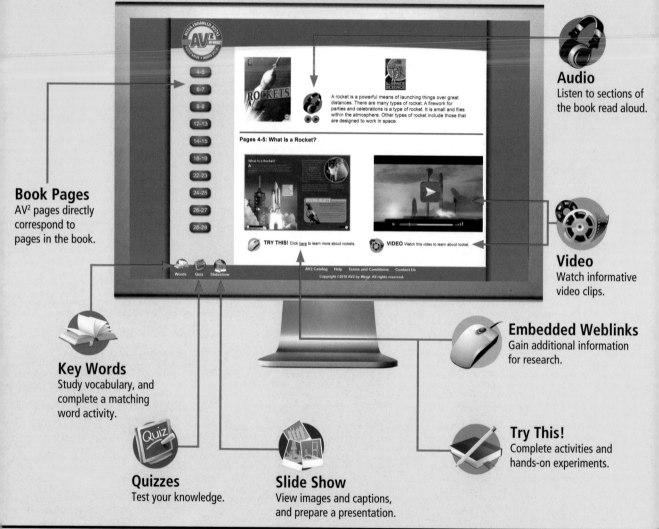

Audio
Listen to sections of the book read aloud.

Book Pages
AV² pages directly correspond to pages in the book.

Video
Watch informative video clips.

Key Words
Study vocabulary, and complete a matching word activity.

Embedded Weblinks
Gain additional information for research.

Try This!
Complete activities and hands-on experiments.

Quizzes
Test your knowledge.

Slide Show
View images and captions, and prepare a presentation.

AV² was built to bridge the gap between print and digital. We encourage you to tell us what you like and what you want to see in the future.

Sign up to be an AV² Ambassador at www.av2books.com/ambassador.

Due to the dynamic nature of the Internet, some of the URLs and activities provided as part of AV² by Weigl may have changed or ceased to exist. AV² by Weigl accepts no responsibility for any such changes. All media enhanced books are regularly monitored to update addresses and sites in a timely manner. Contact AV² by Weigl at 1-866-649-3445 or av2books@weigl.com with any questions, comments, or feedback.